WOMEN

of

PURPOSE

JEAN B. BINGHAM

DESERET
BOOK

SALT LAKE CITY, UTAH

Interior images: © Irtsya/Shutterstock.com

ISBN 978-1-62972-743-1

Printed in the United States of America
Artistic Printing, Salt Lake City, UT

10 9 8 7 6 5 4 3 2 1

Since I was small, I have loved to watch the night sky and try to pick out familiar constellations. If you look up into the sky on a clear night, you can see glowing planets and twinkling stars. On some nights, you will see the moon; on others, you may see a meteor or shooting star as it scoots across the sky. Depending on the amount of light in the night environment, whether you are in a brightly lit parking lot in the middle of town or out in an uninhabited area, you may see just a smattering of very bright stars or an incredible array of stars dusting the velvet expanse—stars so numerous it boggles the mind.

From the darkest parts of Earth, the naked human eye can see about 5,000 stars; from a brightly lit city street, only about 100 stars are visible. A few years ago, astronomers in Australia used some of the world's most powerful instruments to calculate how many stars are actually in the entire visible universe. From their measurements, they concluded that there are 70 sextillion stars—or seven followed by twenty-two zeroes—and some scientists say the actual count could be much, much bigger still.[1]

Does that make you feel small? Contemplating that incredible number fills me with a humble yet exhilarating realization that, among all that vastness, our Father in Heaven knows not only *where* I am but *who* I am and *what* I am thinking and doing and struggling with. And He knows everything about *you*, too, and loves you more than you can even comprehend.

God's capacity for knowledge and love is infinite; His interest is personal and intimate and real. You are valued by Heavenly Parents because you are Their offspring—Their reason for joy. Their purpose is our progress. After all, Their work and glory is to bring about our immortality and eternal life (see Moses 1:39).

Each individual is not only valued but essential in God's plan of happiness. Among all those millions and billions and quadrillions of stars, no two are exactly alike. They differ in brightness and color, in size and location, in age and mass—and they are all important in God's design. It may help to remember that when sometimes we may feel we don't fit in or we don't have much to contribute or our particular talents are not needed.

As those who know me well are aware, my own story is quite "ordinary." Growing up, although I enjoyed learning, I was not the top student in any class. I cannot boast of any expert skills. I play the piano, but only enough to stumble through a hymn. I love to visit art museums to see the paintings and sculptures by great masters, yet my artistic talents were limited to doodling designs in my notebooks. I learned to sew a wearable skirt, but tailoring a suit was definitely beyond my ability. Although I was blessed with good health and loved to run through the park or swim in the lake, I didn't participate in school sports at any level. I was never asked to the prom, I wasn't the president of anything, I was never one of the popular group, and one strikingly attractive friend said to me after scrutinizing my features, "Well, you'll never be beautiful, but you could be cute." In other words, I was just average.

Some of you may relate to these kinds of experiences, feeling that you are also "just average." If you're human—and particularly, a female human—you have probably experienced those times of self-doubt and discouragement that you are not all that you want to be. However, from our Heavenly Parents' perfect perspective, each one of Their children has been created for a divine purpose, has infinite worth, and has a vital work to accomplish in this life.

Even in my "ordinariness," Heavenly Father saw value and has helped me begin to develop the gifts and graces He knows will help me become all that He has designed me to be. Know that your Heavenly Father will provide all that *you* need to become "extra"-ordinary as a daughter of God. The wonder of His heavenly economy is that every single one of us can be spectacular because of our unique bundle of talents and abilities. Unlike the world, in His kingdom there is no winner's platform that has room for only one or two. *Each* of His daughters has been taught and prepared and gifted premortally with marvelous potential to become a queen in the celestial kingdom.

What do you want to accomplish in your life? What are your goals and aspirations? If your long-term goal is to enter the celestial kingdom to live with our Heavenly Parents and with loved family members forever, that singular focus will take you farther than you now think is possible. We are promised, "Eye hath not seen, nor ear heard, neither have entered into the heart of man [or woman], the things which God hath prepared for them that love him" (1 Corinthians 2:9).

You have incredible potential for good because you are a covenant daughter of Heavenly Parents. The evidence of your inherent potential for greatness is the simple fact that you were born on the earth because you made the choice in the premortal world to accept Heavenly Father's plan of salvation and to follow the example of His Son, Jesus Christ. I believe we each made promises to our Heavenly Parents to build on what we learned while we lived with Them and to continue to strive to become like Them. Not one spirit was created to fail; every single one has the capacity to triumph. It is up to us individually to make the choices that bring us closer to that potential.

Unfortunately, one of Heavenly Father's most advanced spirit sons chose the way of pride and forever lost the opportunity to become a god. In his anger and jealousy, he and those he convinced to follow him work tirelessly to confuse us, to deceive us, to discourage us, and to distract us from fulfilling our divine roles and highest potential.

But because Jesus Christ was willing to take upon Himself the sins and infirmities—or inadequacies—of each of us (see Alma 7:11–13), and fulfilled that sacred trust through His infinite Atonement, we can have every confidence that we can become all we were divinely designed to be. As we make and keep sacred covenants, we demonstrate our desire to fulfill that divine potential.

Answer this question: Do you think our Heavenly Parents want us to succeed? Yes! They want us to succeed gloriously! And do you think They will help us? Absolutely! We know that God's "work and glory is to bring to pass the immortality"—which has already been accomplished through the Savior's Atonement and Resurrection—"and eternal life of man" (Moses 1:39). His goal is for every single one of us to return to our eternal home, having increased the talents and gifts with which He blesses us through our obedience and perseverance during this mortal life. We know we cannot do this on our own, but through Heavenly Father's love and the Savior's grace, we can accomplish all that is required for exaltation.

One beautiful spring day I left the door open to enjoy the fresh air. A small bird flew in the open door and then realized this was not where it wanted to be. It flew desperately around the room, repeatedly flying into the window glass in an attempt to escape. I tried to gently guide it toward the open door, but it was frightened and kept darting away. It finally landed on top of the window drapes in bewildered exhaustion. I took a broom and slowly reached the bristle end up to where the bird nervously perched. As I held the head of the broom next to its feet, the bird tentatively stepped onto the bristles.

Slowly, very slowly, I walked to the open door, holding the broom as steady as I could. As soon as we reached the open door, the bird swiftly flew to freedom.

Like that bird, sometimes we are afraid to trust because we don't understand God's absolute love and desire to help us. But when we study Heavenly Father's plan and Jesus Christ's mission, we understand that Their only objective is our eternal happiness and progress. They delight to help us when we ask, seek, and knock (see Matthew 7:7). When we exercise faith and humbly open ourselves to Their answers, we become free from the constraints of our misunderstandings and assumptions, and we can be shown the way forward.

That thought sustained me when I was called as General President of the Relief Society. Knowing that I did not have all the wisdom and ability to fulfill what would be required, I nevertheless took comfort and strength from the knowledge that God "has all wisdom, and all power, both in heaven and in earth" (Mosiah 4:9), and if we just try, just do our best, imperfect as that will be, the Lord will be "on [our] right hand and on [our] left, and [angels will] bear [us] up" (Doctrine and Covenants 84:88). All He requires is "the heart and a willing mind" (Doctrine and Covenants 64:34), and as we are obedient to His commandments, we will be strengthened to accomplish all that is required in this life as well as for entrance into His kingdom in the life hereafter. That choice to become a disciple of Christ gives us the opportunity to wield a more-than-might-be-expected influence on those around us.

Sisters, every one of us has this same promise and potential. It matters not where we live, the makeup of our family, the size of our bank account, whether we are a world-class expert in some field, or how long we have been a member of the Church—we can each be a powerful influence for good. Living with integrity at home and in the community, using a gentle voice and kind words with a challenging child or difficult coworker, demonstrating your standards by your modest way of dressing, reaching out of your comfort zone to become acquainted with those who live around you—there are many simple actions we can do that will influence others to also rise to a higher plane.

Going back to our analogy of the stars: stars produce heat, light, and various forms of radiation that influence their celestial neighbors.[2] Like the stars that are each placed in a particular orbit and location, we have an influence on those around us. Because you are unique, there are things only you can do in your particular way to bless your eternal sisters and brothers. You must make the effort to grow and learn and develop those unique talents and characteristics that contribute to the eternal progress of yourself and others.

I recently read this statement by a woman leader of the Church. Who do you think said this? "Never have women had greater influence than in today's world. Never have the doors of opportunity opened wider for them. This is an inviting, exciting, challenging, and demanding period of time for women. It is a time rich in rewards if we keep our balance, learn the true values of life, and wisely determine priorities."[3] That was Belle S. Spafford, in 1974, who was the Relief Society General President for almost thirty years! Interestingly, her statement is just as true today.

So, what will we do with this time of great opportunity and challenge? "How vast *is* our purpose, how broad is our mission"?[4]

Those of you who are familiar with the history of the settlement of frontier areas around the world know that many towns began as haphazard gatherings of rough men who came to do business and find their fortunes. It wasn't until women arrived in increasing numbers and insisted on establishing churches and schools and an orderly environment that real progress was made on what could be called civilized living. Elder D. Todd Christofferson explained this process and the reasons why: "From age immemorial, societies have relied on the moral force of women. While certainly not the only positive influence at work in society, the moral foundation provided by women has proved uniquely beneficial to the common good. Perhaps, because it is pervasive, this contribution of women is often underappreciated. . . . Women bring with them into the world a certain virtue, a divine gift that makes them adept at instilling such qualities as faith, courage, empathy, and refinement in relationships and in cultures."[5]

Women are given gifts that allow them to see the details as well as the big picture, often at the same time. Discover those gifts and use them, dear sisters!

I remember President James E. Faust telling us in his rich yet humble voice: "You sisters do not know the full extent of your influence. You sisters enrich all of humanity. . . . Each woman brings her own separate, unique strengths to the family and the Church. Being a daughter of God means that if you seek it, you can find your true identity. You will know who you are. This will make you free—not free from restraints, but free from doubts, anxieties, or peer pressure. You will not need to worry, 'Do I look all right?' 'Do I sound OK?' 'What do people think of me?' A conviction that you are a daughter of God gives you a feeling of comfort in your self-worth. It means that you can find strength in the balm of Christ. It will help you meet the heartaches and challenges with faith and serenity."[6]

So, who *are* we as Relief Society sisters? Although each woman is unique, there are feelings and divine gifts and experiences that we have in common that bind us together. We are daughters of our Heavenly Parents, who love us and want us to become like Them. We are full partners with our brethren in the work of salvation—the saving of the souls of men and women—which is the focus of all our efforts. As sisters and brothers, we were given and accepted responsibilities in the premortal world for building the kingdom of God on the earth. Speaking of the "noble and great ones" (that's you!), "even before they were born, they, with many others, received their first lessons in the world of spirits and were prepared to come forth in the due time of the Lord to labor in his vineyard for the salvation of the souls of men" (Doctrine and Covenants 138:55–56).

As Emma Smith, the first Relief Society General President, phrased it in 1842, "We are going to do something extraordinary."[7] You may not realize it yet, but Relief Society can help you accomplish extraordinary things.

What does Relief Society mean to *you*? As adult female members of The Church of Jesus Christ of Latter-day Saints, you and I belong to one of the oldest and largest women's organizations in the world. With more than 7.4 million sisters around the globe, we have a bond that can be eternal.

Relief Society is more than a class on Sunday. "It is a divinely established sisterhood. . . . [It] is a place of learning. . . . It is an organization whose basic charter is caring for others,"[8] as expressed in our motto, "Charity Never Faileth." It is a safe place for sisters to bring their questions and for those who are searching for identity and purpose. It is a place that will help us blossom individually and improve collectively.

What does Relief Society mean to me? Relief Society has changed over the years—and has changed *me* over the years! To paraphrase, "It's not just your grandma's Relief Society." When I left home to go to college, I automatically became a member of Relief Society. I gathered with other young women my age to learn the gospel and to serve others in an organized way. My first callings were as a Relief Society teacher and a visiting teacher. It was easy to knock on the door of an apartment in my complex and to chat with the girls who were of my similar age and circumstance.

Later, as a brand-new mother, I was called to teach Relief Society mother education classes. My circle was expanded as the women in my new ward accepted me with open hearts and provided great examples. I found role models in faithful sisters who valued motherhood and delighted in their role as well as in those who were pursuing education or were employed and established in a career. It was more challenging to visit teach because of the distances involved, but I was blessed to be visited by women who genuinely cared about me and showed me how to extend that love to other sisters who were in different stages of life from mine.

As a more mature (read "aging") woman, my circle has been expanded yet again to include many younger than myself. Now I am the "experienced" one who can share my hard-earned insights as well as be invigorated by younger sisters who are enthusiastic about what lies ahead. Over the years, I have learned to be persistent in contacting all the sisters whom I have been given to visit—including those who have not been as involved in the Church—and because of our common experiences as women, I have found wonderful friends who have enriched my life. As I work to express the Savior's love through serving them in ways that are meaningful to them, their hearts soften, and they often become receptive to the Spirit.

There have also been bumps and challenges along the way. Not every interaction at Relief Society has been perfect. There have been women who were insensitive to my feelings, who didn't respond to me in a Christlike way. And on the other hand, I'm sure I have been the cause of unintended hurt to some of my sisters in the gospel. One experience was so painful that I wanted to move to another city to avoid any more trauma and drama! Yet each time, in remembering the example of our Savior, Jesus Christ, the "eyes of [my] understanding were opened" (Doctrine and Covenants 110:1), and through His grace I came to genuinely love and enjoy those sisters who had heretofore been difficult for me to appreciate.

I learned a lesson on misunderstandings when three-year-old Alyssa, who was watching a movie with her siblings, remarked with a puzzled expression, "Mom, that chicken is weird!"

Her mother looked at the screen and responded with a smile, "Honey, that is a peacock."

Like that unknowing three-year-old, we sometimes look at others with an incomplete or inaccurate understanding. We may focus on the differences and perceived flaws in those around us, whereas our Heavenly Father sees His children, created in His eternal image, with magnificent and glorious potential.

President James E. Faust is remembered to have said, "The older I get, the less judgmental I become."⁹ That reminds me of the Apostle Paul's observation: "When I was a child, I spake as a child, I understood as a child, I thought as a child: but when I became [older], I put away childish things. For now we see through a glass, darkly; but then face to face: now I know in part; but then shall I know even as also I am known" (1 Corinthians 13:11–12).

When we see our own imperfections more clearly, we are less inclined to view others "through a glass, darkly." We want to use the light of the gospel to see others as the Savior does—with compassion, hope, and charity. The day will come when we will have a complete understanding of others' hearts and will be grateful to have mercy extended to us—just as we extend charitable thoughts and words to others during this life.

So what do we *do* as Relief Society sisters? If you are familiar with the updated Relief Society purpose statement, you know that "Relief Society helps prepare women for the blessings of eternal life as they increase faith in Heavenly Father and Jesus Christ and His Atonement; [as they] strengthen individuals, families, and homes through ordinances and covenants; and [as they] work in unity to help those in need."¹⁰

So, number one, we work to fulfill our divine potential. To do that, we "all work together" to love, "to cheer and to bless in [the Savior's] name."¹¹ We participate in the work of salvation, which "includes member missionary work, convert retention, activation of less-active members, temple and family history work, and teaching the gospel"[12]—all things which you are already doing. All baptized members of the Church, including children, participate in this work, which is accomplished with steady effort, a bit at a time, in the family and the workplace or school, the neighborhood and the community—anywhere and everywhere we have an influence.

Sometimes we think we have to do something grand and heroic to "count" as serving our neighbors. Yet simple acts of service can have profound effects on others—as well as on ourselves. What did the Savior do? Through His supernal gifts of the Atonement and Resurrection, "none other has had so profound an influence [on] all who have lived and who will yet live upon the earth."[13] But He also smiled at, talked with, walked with, listened to, made time for, encouraged, taught, fed, and forgave. He served family and friends, neighbors and strangers alike, and He invited acquaintances and loved ones to enjoy the rich blessings of His gospel. Those "simple" acts of service and love provide a template for our work today.

As we put our arm around a shy sister at church, as we reach out to a young woman who is struggling, as we work to feed and clothe and teach a child on a daily basis, as we share what makes us happy about the restored gospel with our neighbor, as we mourn with someone who has lost a loved one, as we attend the temple at an inconvenient time, as we help a refugee navigate the bewildering array in a grocery store, as we expend effort in learning and developing our talents with the goal of being an instrument for the Lord, as we patiently tutor a new member who is learning to do family history, as we prepare to teach a Primary or seminary class—all of these actions and many more acts of simple but meaningful service are part of the work of salvation. *That* is our mission, and it truly is vast, but it *is doable* when we each do something—and keep at it!

For instance, a busy young mother in Arizona wondered what she could do to help a newly arrived refugee family in her community in some small way. She soon learned that she could help furnish a few articles for their empty apartment. When she and her children visited the family to bring the articles, she realized that the mother had no purse to carry her personal items. And a woman needs a purse! She knew that she and many of her friends had extra purses that could be useful to these women, so she sent out a request on social media. That simple beginning has blossomed into a warehouse full of items needed by just-arriving families and has also become the means of providing many community members with a welcome opportunity to give of themselves, as well as created a sweet bond between these women of different faiths.

Perhaps I can explain more about the blessings of simple service with an analogy. Some years ago, I went canoeing with a group of young women. The deep blue lakes surrounded by green, thickly forested hills and rocky cliffs were breathtakingly beautiful. The water sparkled on our paddles as we dipped them into the clear water, and the sun shone warmly while we moved smoothly across the lake.

However, clouds soon darkened the sky, and a stiff wind began to blow. To make any progress at all, we had to dig deeply into the water, paddling without pausing between strokes. After a few grueling hours of backbreaking work, we finally turned the corner on the large lake and discovered to our amazement and delight that the wind was blowing in the direction we wanted to go.

Quickly, we took advantage of this gift. We pulled out a small tarp and tied two of its corners to paddle handles and the other corners to my husband's feet, which he stretched out over the gunwales of the canoe. The wind billowed the improvised sail, and we were off!

When the young women in the other canoes saw how we moved along the water with ease, they quickly improvised sails of their own. Our hearts were light with laughter and relief, grateful for the respite from the challenges of the day.

How like that glorious wind can be the sincere compliment of a friend, the cheerful greeting of a parent, the approving nod of a sibling, or the helpful smile of a coworker or classmate, all supplying fresh "wind in our sails" as we battle the challenges of life! President Thomas S. Monson put it this way: "We can't direct the wind, but we can adjust the sails. For maximum happiness, peace, and contentment, may we *choose* a positive attitude."[14]

Words have surprising power, both to build up and to tear down. We can all probably remember negative words that brought us low and other words spoken with love that made our spirits soar. Choosing to say only that which is positive about—and to—others lifts and strengthens those around us and helps others follow in the Savior's way.

Sister Eliza R. Snow, the second General President of the Relief Society, testified, "If any of the daughters and mothers in Israel are feeling in the least [limited] in their present spheres, they will now find ample scope for every power and capability for doing good with which they are most liberally endowed."[15]

So, what "extraordinary thing" will you choose to do? Choose something according to your available time and resources. "Do not run faster or labor more than you have strength and means; . . . but be diligent" (Doctrine and Covenants 10:4). Whether your "work of salvation" is largely in the home at this time in life or your influence extends to a global scale, or somewhere in between, the Lord is pleased with your efforts when you are focused on serving God's children and the eternal goal of returning to Him as a "new and improved" version of your spiritual self. As Elder Dieter F. Uchtdorf phrased it so succinctly, "Exaltation is our goal; discipleship is our journey."[16]

As we go forward in this journey of discipleship, may we each determine to reach out in small and simple ways that bless our families and others in "extraordinary" ways. May we treasure our relationships in this divinely designed organization and come to know and follow Jesus Christ, whose teachings and perfect example will lead us back to our Heavenly Father.

NOTES

1 See Andrew Craig, "Astronomers count the stars," *BBC News*, July 22, 2003; news.bbc.co.uk/2/hi/science/nature/3085885.stm.

2 See Catherine Zuckerman, "Everything you wanted to know about stars," *National Geographic* online, March 20, 2019; www.nationalgeographic.com/science/space/universe/stars/.

3 Belle S. Spafford, *A Woman's Reach* (1974), 21.

4 Emily H. Woodmansee, "As Sisters in Zion," *Hymns of The Church of Jesus Christ of Latter-day Saints* (1985), no. 309.

5 D. Todd Christofferson, "The Moral Force of Women," *Ensign*, November 2013.

6 James E. Faust, "What It Means to Be a Daughter of God," *Ensign*, November 1999.

7 See *Daughters in My Kingdom: The History and Work of Relief Society* (2011), 14.

8 James E. Faust, "What It Means to Be a Daughter of God."

9 As quoted in Dallin H. Oaks, "'Judge Not' and Judging," *Ensign*, August 1999.

10 *Handbook 2: Administering the Church* (2019), 9.1.1.

11 Woodmansee, "As Sisters in Zion," *Hymns*, no. 309.

12 *Handbook 2*, Section 5 introduction.

13 "The Living Christ: The Testimony of the Apostles," *Ensign*, May 2017.

14 Thomas S. Monson, "Living the Abundant Life," *Ensign*, January 2012.

15 See *Daughters in My Kingdom*, 44.

16 Dieter F. Uchtdorf, "It Works Wonderfully!" *Ensign*, November 2015.